Better Homes and Gardens®

BUGS, BUGS, BUGS

Hi! My name is Max. I have some great projects to show you—and they're all about bugs! We're going to have lots of fun making them together.

Inside You'll Find...

Bugs in the Air

Max enjoys rowing a boat on the pond in his favorite park.
He likes looking for the friendly dragonflies that live around the
water. Can you point to the 8 dragonflies?

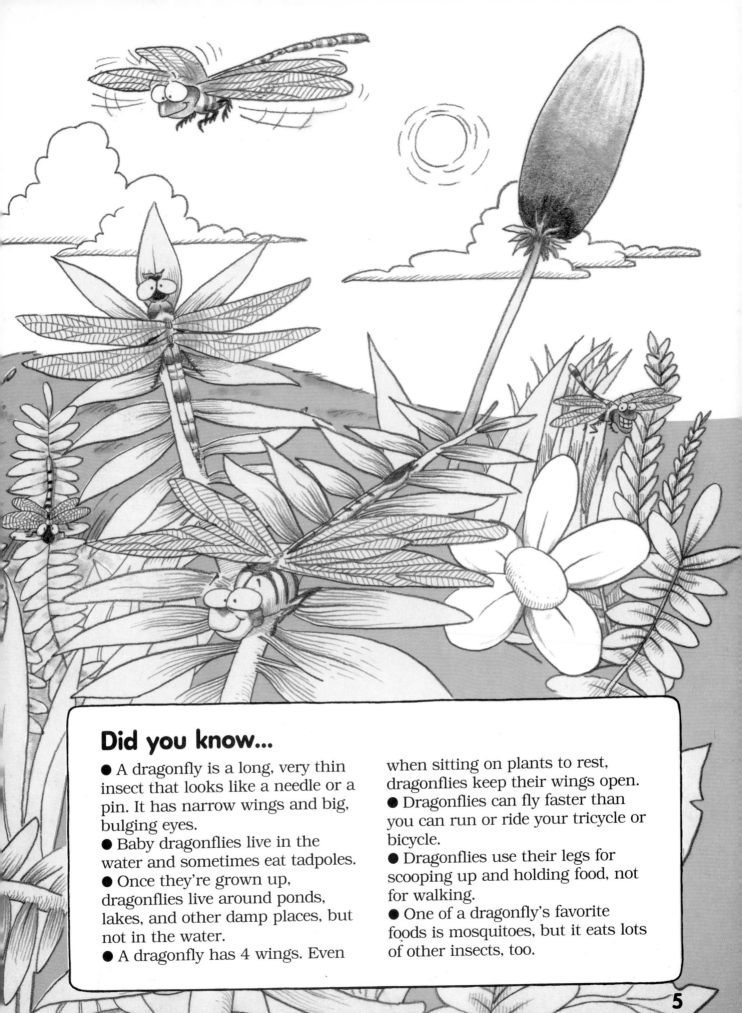

Did you know...

● A dragonfly is a long, very thin insect that looks like a needle or a pin. It has narrow wings and big, bulging eyes.

● Baby dragonflies live in the water and sometimes eat tadpoles.

● Once they're grown up, dragonflies live around ponds, lakes, and other damp places, but not in the water.

● A dragonfly has 4 wings. Even when sitting on plants to rest, dragonflies keep their wings open.

● Dragonflies can fly faster than you can run or ride your tricycle or bicycle.

● Dragonflies use their legs for scooping up and holding food, not for walking.

● One of a dragonfly's favorite foods is mosquitoes, but it eats lots of other insects, too.

Design bugs from clothespins.

Rainbow Dragonflies

Make a bunch of colorful, fluttering dragonflies. Then fly them around in your hand or use thread to hang them in a window.

What you'll need...

- Construction paper
- Table knife
- Pencil
- Scissors
- Clothespins
- Dragonfly Decorations (see tip on page 7)
- Tape
- Thread or string

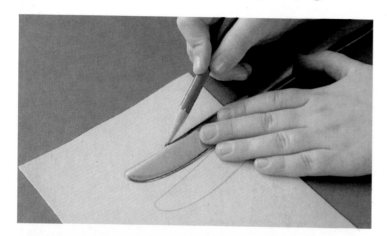

1 For the wings, fold a sheet of construction paper in half. Lay the top of the table knife flat on the paper. Trace around the knife onto the paper. Move the knife and trace it again, right next to the first drawing (see photo). Cut out the wings, keeping them attached.

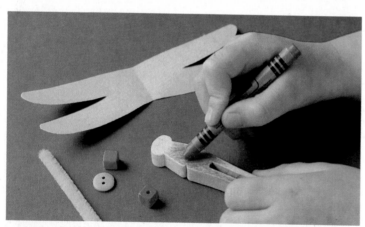

2 Decorate the clothespin and wings with crayons or any of the other Dragonfly Decorations.

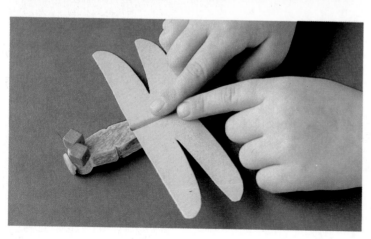

3 Place the wings, folded side down, in the slit of the clothespin. Press wings open (see photo). Tape the wings to the clothespin.

   If you would like to hang your dragonfly in a window, tie a piece of thread around the clothespin just in front of the wings (see photo on page 7).

Dragonfly Decorations

To make beautiful bugs:
● Color the clothespin and wings with crayons, markers, or tempera paint.
● Or, glue on glitter.
● For the eyes, glue on shiny beads or buttons.
● Look around the house for other decorations such as paper fasteners, yarn, pipe cleaners, or foil.

A paper-plate insect becomes a counting friend.

Magic Number Bug

This pretty ladybug has wings that move up and down. Count the number of dots and write that number under its wings.

What you'll need...

- Scissors
- Three 7-inch paper plates
- Construction paper
- White crafts glue
- Pencil
- Paper fastener
- Tape
- Markers, crayons, stickers, or buttons

1 For the ladybug's wings, cut the first plate in half (see photo). For the head, cut out the round center from the second plate. Cut two small strips of construction paper and glue onto the head for antennae.

2 With adult help, use a pencil to poke a hole in the third plate. Also, poke a hole at the top of each wing. Make holes about ½ inch from the edge.

Place the wings on top of the third plate (ladybug's body). Push a paper fastener through the holes to hold the plate and wings together (see photo). Press the fastener open.

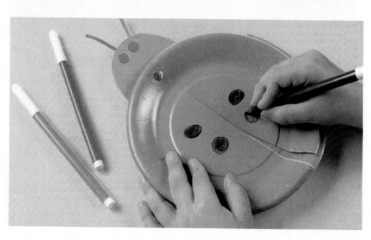

3 Tape the head of the ladybug to the back of the third plate. Decorate your ladybug any way you like. Draw dots on the ladybug's wings (see photo). Count the dots and write the number on the plate (ladybug's body) hidden underneath the ladybug's wings.

Max helps identify the different types of rooms in an ant house.

Bugs on the Ground

Arnold the Ant just got home. His friends are in underground rooms throughout their ant house. Which room should he go to for a visit with the queen? What's your favorite room? Why?

Nursery

Dining Room

Bedroom

Queen's Room

New Room

Garbage Room

Living Room

Did you know...

● Ants live in groups called colonies (KOL-uh-nees). Some colonies have only a few ants and others have thousands of ants!

● The ants' home is called a nest and is often underground.

● Most ant homes have several rooms. Each room is for something special, like taking care of baby ants or storing food. Can you find the 7 rooms in the drawing?

● There are 3 kinds of ants in each colony—the queen, the males, and the workers.

● The worker ants take care of the queen, hunt for food, take care of baby ants, or build and protect the nest.

● You can tell which ants are the worker ants because they don't have wings. The queen and the male ants have wings.

Fancy Ants

Go ahead—invite these cute ants to a picnic lunch. They won't eat the food off your plate because they're made from paper. And guess what. You can make them creepy crawly!

What you'll need...

- Crazy Ants (see tip on page 13)
- Scissors
- Pencil
- Paper fasteners (magnet-attracting)
- Crayons, markers, or colored pencils
- Paper plate
- Small magnet

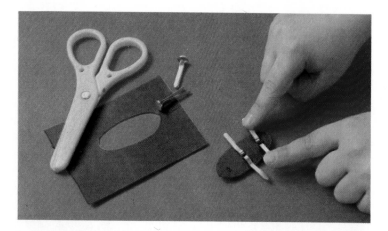

1 Make a Crazy Ant body. With adult help, use a pencil to poke 3 holes in the ant body. For the legs, place 2 paper fasteners into 2 holes next to each other. Bend the points so they lie flat (see photo). Turn the ant over. For the antennae, place another fastener, point side up, in last hole. Bend back slightly.

2 Make as many ants as you like. Draw some food on a paper plate for your ants to "eat" (see photo).

Put the ants on the plate. Place the magnet underneath the plate near one of the ants. Make the ant crawl by moving your magnet around the plate.

Crazy Ants

Black, blue, even red—
make your Fancy Ants any
color you like.

For the ant body, cut a
small oblong shape (about
as big as a peanut shell)
from construction paper.
Cut curves along the sides,
if you want.

A sandwich box transforms into a roving, funny-looking bug.

Scooter Bug

Do you know what scoots, scampers, and scurries across the floor? Why, it's a homemade box bug. Make two and have a race!

What you'll need...

- Crafts knife or sharp paring knife
- Small plastic foam box
- Two pipe cleaners
- Bug Decorations (see tip on page 15)
- Whole lemon

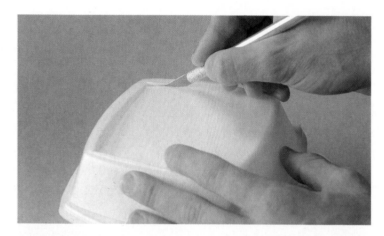

1 With adult help, cut the bottom out of the plastic foam box.

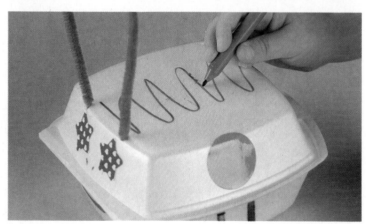

2 To make the antennae, stick the pipe cleaners into the top of the box. Use the Bug Decorations on the box any way you like (see photo).

Place the lemon underneath the box. Place the box on a smooth floor and give it a push. Watch your Scooter Bug go!

14

Bug Decorations

What kind of Scooter Bug are you going to make?

● Use markers to draw lines or spots all over your plastic foam box bug.

● Or, decorate it with adhesive stickers and make a tongue out of ribbon.

● Or, cut out pieces of colorful construction paper. Then glue or tape them onto your Scooter Bug.

A simple sketch becomes a challenging puzzle.

Stick-Puzzle Pals

Question: What can you make with crafts sticks, crayons, and tape? Answer: A Stick-Puzzle Pal, that's what!

What you'll need...
● Jumbo crafts sticks
● Tape
● Crayons or markers

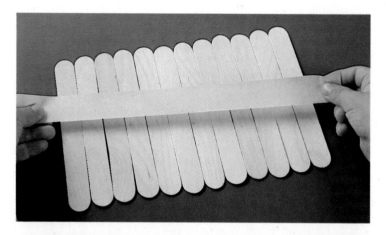

1 Place crafts sticks side by side so that they touch. Use as many sticks as you like. Line the sticks up evenly.

Cut a piece of tape that's longer than the stick bundle. Lay the tape across the middle of the sticks (see photo). Press down firmly. This holds the sticks together.

2 Turn the sticks over. Using crayons make a drawing on the sticks (see photo). If you like, write your name, numbers, or letters on the sticks.

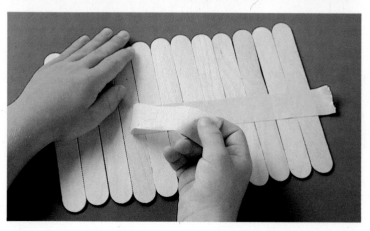

3 Turn the sticks over. Pull the tape off the back of the sticks (see photo). Now, mix up the sticks and put the puzzle back together again.

Name the objects that begin with the letter B.

Beautiful Butterflies

Max and his best friend, Elliot, are taking a nature walk through a meadow. They see several butterflies. How many other things that start with the letter B can you find in the picture?

Did you know...

- A female butterfly lays eggs that hatch into caterpillars.
- As soon as a caterpillar hatches, it begins to eat. It eats almost constantly and has to shed its skin many times because it grows so fast.

- When the caterpillar is fully grown, it stops eating and gets ready to turn into a butterfly.

  Some caterpillars spin a silk cocoon around their bodies and hang from something like a branch. Other caterpillars dig a hole in the ground to hide.

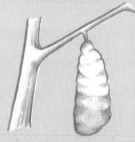

- The caterpillar sleeps for weeks or months inside the silky cocoon or in the ground.

- While the caterpillar sleeps, its body changes. When it comes out of the cocoon, it's not a caterpillar anymore—it's a beautiful butterfly!

Thread a shoestring through rigatoni to make bug jewelry.

Caterpillar Necklace

Have you ever worn a caterpillar around your neck? You can!
Use pasta, paper, and a shoestring to make a wiggly necklace.

What you'll need...

- Small paper cup or nut cup
- Pencil
- Construction paper
- Scissors
- Neat Necklaces (see tip on page 21)
- About 36 inches of shoestring, ribbon, or yarn
- Uncooked rigatoni
- Tape
- Two 3-inch pieces of ribbon

1 Using the cup as a guide, draw 8 circles on the construction paper (see photo). Cut out the circles. With adult help, use a pencil to poke a hole in the center of each paper circle.

For the caterpillar's head, draw a face on one of the circles. Decorate the rest of the circles any way you like.

2 Thread one of the paper circles on the shoestring. Then thread a piece of rigatoni on the shoestring (see photo). Repeat, threading the circles and rigatoni until they are all on the shoestring.

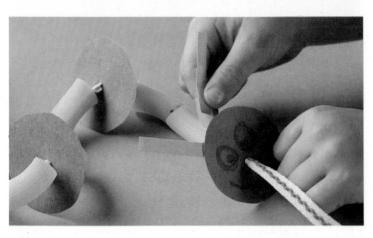

3 To make antennae, tape the ribbon to the head of the caterpillar (see photo). Tie the ends of the shoestring together. Your necklace is ready to wear!

Neat Necklaces

It's easy to make other kinds of bug necklaces.
● Cut the circles from several different colors of construction paper.
● Or, make only 2 paper circles—1 for the head and 1 for the end. Use all pasta to make the body.
● Or, skip the pasta and make a necklace using cut-up drinking straws.

A lip-smacking butterfly made from pretzels and candy.

Fluttering Butterflies

These butterflies are both pretty and scrumptious to eat!
Use pretzels for the wings and colorful candy for the body.

What you'll need...

- Table knife
- Gumdrops or candied orange slices
- Pretzels
- Assorted candy
- Canned frosting

1 For the body, cut two slits in a gumdrop.

2 For the wings, press 1 pretzel into each slit.

3 Decorate your butterfly with assorted candy (see photo). Use the frosting to help "glue" the candy to the butterfly.

A searching and matching game for different types of insects.

Ugly Bugs

Shhhh! Max is looking for crickets, beetles, and mosquitoes in the tall grass. Can you help him find the 9 ugly bugs in the picture? Which bug do you like best? Why?

Mosquito

Cricket

Beetle

Now that you've found all the bugs, point to the ones that look alike.

Did you know...

● Crickets, mosquitoes, and beetles are all insects, but they look different from each other.

● Crickets rub their wings together to make noise. Only male crickets make this sound. Have you ever heard a cricket make this chirping sound?

● Crickets have ears. Your ears are on your head, but their ears are on their front legs!

● Mosquitoes have needlelike mouths and tiny hairs all over their bodies. Some of these hairs act like ears.

● Only female mosquitoes make noise and bite. After biting you, the mosquito sucks up some of your blood. Has a mosquito ever bitten you?

● There are more beetles in the world than any other type of insect.

● Look closely at a beetle and you may be able to see that it has a mouth with jaws. It looks a little like your mouth!

Easy-to-make cookies that look like bugs.

Best Bug Cookies

Shape the brown and white cookie dough into cute, crawly bugs. Decorate them, bake them, and best of all, eat them!

What you'll need...

- Best Bug Cookie Dough (see page 32)
- Cookie Decorations (see tip on page 27)

1 Spoon the dough onto an ungreased cookie sheet (see photo). Gently press the dough with your fingers to shape into different kinds of bugs.

2 Decorate your bug cookies any way you like (see Cookie Decorations tip).

   With adult help, bake the cookies as directed on page 32.

Max likes to keep his cookies tasting fresh. So he stores them in a container with a tight-fitting lid. Sometimes he puts a piece of waxed paper between each layer of cookies.

WAXED PAPER

Cookie Decorations

There are lots of goodies you can use to decorate your bug cookies.

Assorted nuts, dry cereals, miniature semisweet chocolate pieces, currants, raisins, coconut, and wheat germ are a few yummy ideas. What would you like to use to decorate your cookies?

Fun-to-wear bug glasses made from egg cartons.

Bug Eyes

Make believe you're a funny-looking bug with these teriffic-looking egg carton goggles. What kind of bug will you be?

What you'll need...

- Scissors
- 2 egg carton cups, attached
- Pencil
- 2 pipe cleaners
- Markers

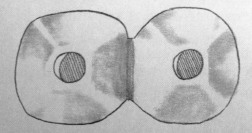

1 Cut the ends out of the egg cups to make eye holes.

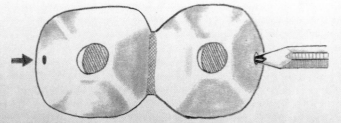

2 With adult help, use a pencil to poke a hole in each side of the attached egg cups.

28

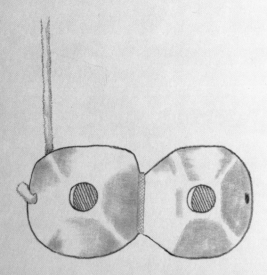

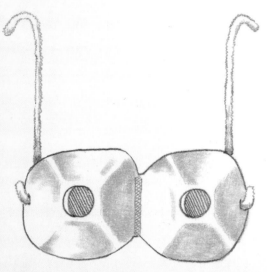

3 Push a pipe cleaner through the hole in each side and twist to hold.

4 Curve pipe cleaners so they will fit behind your ears. Decorate your Bug Eyes with markers any way you like.

Parents' Pages

We've filled this special section with more activities, recipes, reading suggestions, hints we learned from our kid-testers, and many more helpful tips.

Bugs in the Air

See pages 4 and 5

To observe dragonflies, you and your children will need to visit a pond or a marshy area. Children are fascinated by how quickly these insects dart around. Did you know that damselflies look a lot like dragonflies? Tell your children this simple way to tell the two bugs apart: If the wings are spread open when it's resting, it's a dragonfly. But if the wings are folded up, it's a damselfly.

Rainbow Dragonflies

See pages 6 and 7

Colorful wrapping paper makes pretty wings. All it takes is a small piece, so save little scraps from presents.

To make a simple bug mobile, use thread or string to hang several dragonflies from a hanger. Hang the hanger on a curtain rod or from a hook, and then adjust the position of the dragonflies to get the mobile to balance.

Tips for Bug Watching

A Bug Guesthouse

Bugs are fascinating to watch, but sometimes they'll scurry away before you can get close enough to see them. To give kids a closeup view, catch a bug in a small box, bottle, or jar.

A Bug Search

Acquaint your children with harmless bugs, such as ladybugs, caterpillars, crickets, and grasshoppers, by reviewing a basic insect book. Remind your children not to handle spiders or bugs in water. Once your children know what safe bugs look like, go outside and find a bug. Then, use your hand or a folded piece of paper to gently scoop the bug into the container.

A Short Visit

When you bring a newfound bug friend into your home, keep the visit brief so no harm is done to the insect.

Magic Number Bug

See pages 8 and 9

Paper plates make this project extra simple. If the plates have slick surfaces, use stickers for the dots or draw them on with permanent markers.

Ask your children to point to the dots while counting. The interaction between the finger movement and reciting the numbers helps children learn faster. Or, use bug for simple addition. Have your children count the dots on each wing, teach them how to add these two numbers, and then open the bug to check the answer.

This clever bug project also makes a great party invitation. Write the party facts—what, when, and where—under the wings. Then give to guests.

Or, adapt the Magic Number Bug idea to make pretty valentines from red, pink, and white construction paper cut in heart shapes. For a lacy edge, glue paper doilies to the backs of the valentines (see photo at left).

Bugs on the Ground

See pages 10 and 11

Ask your children if they have ever heard of a snack called "Ants on a Log?" This tasty snack is so easy they can make it themselves. See page 31 for recipe directions.

Ants on a Log

Give your children celery sticks, peanut butter, and raisins. First, show them how to use a table knife to spread the peanut butter into the groove of the celery stick. Next, show them how to place the raisin "ants" on the "log" (see photo). Now it's their turn to try.

Fancy Ants

See pages 12 and 13

When we first made these ants, we used some fasteners that we bought a few years ago only to find that they weren't attracted to the magnet.

So, we took our magnet to the store and found brass-coated, metal fasteners that the magnet could pick up.

When looking for a magnet, check your refrigerator. The small magnets used to hold notes and other papers on the refrigerator door are just what you need. Another common place to find small magnets is in a home workshop.

Scooter Bug

See pages 14 and 15

Our kid-testers raved about this project—they even had a Scooter Bug race. It's a quick and easy craft and it's lots of fun to play with. Use a plastic foam sandwich container from a fast-food restaurant or deli.

Stick-Puzzle Pals

Pages 16 and 17

Crafts sticks come in different sizes. We discovered the jumbo sticks are the easiest for kids to handle.

This is a good puzzle project for helping your children learn letters and numbers. After they draw a simple picture on the sticks, label each stick with a number or a letter.

For example, use a child's name, writing one letter on each stick. Then remove tape, jumble the sticks, and help them put sticks back together.

Beautiful Butterflies

See pages 18 and 19

Besides the four butterflies, the nature walk picture is loaded with things that start with the letter B. Did your kids find: boots, a belt, a buckle, a bear, a bird, a bunny, a bug, a beaver, binoculars, branches, a bandage, and a book? Look at pictures in the box—there's a branch and a butterfly.

● Reading suggestions:
My First Butterflies
   by Cecilia Fitzsimons
The Very Hungry Caterpillar
   by Eric Carle

Monarch

Eastern Black Swallowtail

Caterpillar Necklace

See pages 20 and 21

When your children wear homemade jewelry, ask them to make up a story.

Perhaps they are from a tribe of American Indians, and the necklaces are their tribal jewelry.

Or, maybe they're from outer space, and the necklaces have hidden powers.

Fluttering Butterflies

See pages 22 and 23

As you snack on the finished butterflies, talk with your children about tasting. Discuss how the pretzels are salty tasting and the candy is sweet. Carry it further and mention how the pretzels are crunchy and the candy is chewy.

Ugly Bugs

See pages 24 and 25

Another bug to point out to your children is the grasshopper. Grasshoppers look quite a bit like their cricket cousins except they are green or greenish brown instead of black.

The drawing below shows the body parts of a grasshopper and other similar insects. Point out the various parts to your children and talk about how the grasshopper uses its back legs for jumping.

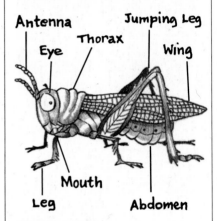

Antenna
Jumping Leg
Eye
Thorax
Wing
Mouth
Leg
Abdomen

Best Bug Cookies

See pages 26 and 27

This project offers four types of fun—mixing the dough, spooning it onto the cookie sheet, adding decorations, and finally, eating the cookies. The bugs start out just as humps of dough. But once they're in the oven, the humps "grow" together to make crazy-looking bugs that taste terrific.

Best Bug Cookie Dough
- ½ cup margarine or butter
- 1¾ cups all-purpose flour
- ½ cup sugar
- ½ cup packed brown sugar
- ¼ cup dairy sour cream
- 1 egg
- 1 teaspoon vanilla
- ½ teaspoon baking soda
- ¼ teaspoon salt
- 1 square (1 ounce) unsweetened chocolate, melted and cooled
  Assorted nuts
  Raisins

● Beat the margarine with an electric mixer on low to medium speed about 30 seconds or till softened.
● Add about half of the flour, the sugar, brown sugar, sour cream, egg, vanilla, baking soda, and salt. Beat on low to medium speed till thoroughly combined, scraping the sides of the bowl often. Then, beat or stir in the remaining flour.
● Divide the dough in half. Stir cooled chocolate into one half. (If dough is sticky, cover and chill about 2 hours.)
● To form bugs, drop vanilla and chocolate dough by rounded teaspoons onto ungreased cookie sheets so that mounds of dough just touch. Keep bugs 3 inches apart.
● Decorate with nuts, raisins, or little blobs of dough.
● Bake in a 375° oven for 8 to 10 minutes or till vanilla part of cookie is golden. Remove from cookie sheets. Cool on wire rack. Makes about 20.

Bugging Bug Eyes

See pages 28 and 29

This simple project takes some preparation on your part. Cut the egg carton before you get your children involved. You can use either paper or plastic foam egg cartons. If you use the plastic foam cartons, use stickers, foil, or permanent markers to decorate.

After the bug eyes are complete, encourage some playacting. Tell your children to make believe they're bugs in the jungle or bugs on the ground. Or, maybe they're flying bugs.

At Halloween, use the bug eyes as part of a bug costume. Dress your children in clothes of one color. Then, add three strips of cloth or masking tape as stripes around their chests. Or, turn the bug eyes into owl's, jack-o'-lantern's, or bat's eyes (see photo).

BETTER HOMES AND GARDENS® BOOKS
Editor: Gerald M. Knox
Art Director: Ernest Shelton
Managing Editor: David A. Kirchner
Department Head, Food and Family Life: Sharyl Heiken

BUGS, BUGS, BUGS
Editors: Sandra Granseth and Diana McMillen
Editorial Project Manager: Liz Anderson
Graphic Designers: Linda Ford Vermie and Brian Wignall
Contributing Illustrator: Buck Jones
Contributing Photographer: Scott Little

Have BETTER HOMES AND GARDENS®
magazine delivered to your door.
For information, write to:
ROBERT AUSTIN
P.O. BOX 4536
DES MOINES, IA. 50336